Who's Our New Teacher?

Written by
Jeanne Willis

Illustrated by
Ben Meadowcroft

The summer holidays were over.
Jack went back to school.

A new teacher was coming.
"I wonder what she'll be like?" said Jack.

"I bet she'll be really **snappy**," said Ben.

"I bet she'll be really creepy," said Jay.

"I bet she'll be really **Silly**," said Kate.

"How do you know?" said Jack.
"I bet she'll be really good."

"Well, my big sister says she's really **batty**," said Jess.

"And my big brother says she's really ratty," said Sam.

"Our new teacher can't be that bad!" said Jack.

"Oh yes, she can!" said Ben and Jay and Kate.

9

"My big sister says she's a **warty toad**," said Jess.

10

"My big brother says she's an **old goat**," said Sam.

11

"Is that her, over there?" said Sam and Jess.
"She's a HORRID MONSTER!"

"That's not her, silly," said Jack.

"Jack's right. That's not her," said Ben …

"Our new teacher will be *much* more **hairy**," said Kate.

"Who told you that?" said Jack.

"My big sister," said Jess.

"My big brother," said Jay.

"My sister says she's not human," said Jess.

"My brother says she comes from **Mars**," said Jay.

The bell rang. It was time to go in.
Time to meet the new teacher!

"You go first," said Jack.

"No, you go first," said Ben and Jay and Kate.

They all went into class …

"Good morning, children!" said a
big green dragon.

"Please, Miss, are you our new teacher?"
said Jack.

"No," said the big green dragon.
"I ate your new teacher."

"She was horrible! Children,
you would have 'ated her too!"

"So now you've got me for the whole term," said the big green dragon, with a **big toothy grin.**

And everyone thought that the big green dragon was their **best** teacher ever!